2.50

TEACHINGS OF INFINITE WISDOM

by

May Clark

Teachings from her spirit guides Pharaoh and Ming Fu

CON-PSY PUBLICATIONS MIDDLESEX

First Edition

Published by

CON-PSY PUBLICATIONS

**22 KINGSLEY AVENUE
SOUTHALL
MIDDLESEX UB1 2NA**

ISBN 1 898680 03 5

Illustrations by Marie Armstrong

DEDICATION

I dedicate this book to my friend and teacher Teresa Doherty, without whose wisdom and guidance the teachings might not have been written. Also to my friend Nancy Cordery, who so generously helped to support me in her sincere desire to be of service to spirit. My deepest thanks to both of them, may the divine spirit bless their pathway.

CONTENTS

FOREWORD

It gives me much pleasure to write this foreword for my friend and pupil, May Clark. May is a dedicated and humble soul who radiates true spiritual beauty, and from whom I have learnt so much by her example.

May has chosen an extremely difficult pathway in this life and has proved herself a genuine servant of God by her willingness to undertake, in true love, burdens which would prove utterly crushing for many of us.

It has been my privilege and joy to help May in the unfoldment of her quite exceptional gifts. She is a medium of the highest calibre and has drawn to her spirit guides of spiritual magnitude and wisdom whose words will greatly enhance the quality of life for many people.

Humility is surely the true hallmark of an evolved soul and it is nowhere better exemplified than in the life of May Clark and in the spiritual stature of her spirit guides.

Teresa Doherty
St. Leonards-on-Sea

September 1993

TEACHINGS FROM

PHARAOH

THE TAPESTRY OF LIFE

Time should not be wasted by living in a state of perplexity, for much knowledge awaits those who desire to learn the true facts of life.

We know from experience how confusing the earth life can be, but I say unto you, allow the light of truth to guide you, to see the wisdom in all things; thus you will learn and understand that God's creation is one of purpose and all His children have a part to play in the great tapestry of life.

Beloved children, turn your face toward the sun and let the shadows fade from your view. By allowing brightness into your life you will dispel the gloom that causes the soul to retreat into a state of melancholy.

Wise men of old have told us that we must learn from the many lessons of life. Each one enables the soul to grow in wisdom; thus beauty will radiate from those who have gained the knowledge the Great Spirit bestows upon us.

All of God's children are given the opportunity to promote soul growth, but they must allow harmonious conditions into their lives, for discord and strife can only mar progress. Remember, dear children of the Great Spirit, your thoughts and deeds are so important, for they create seeds that will perfect or destroy the loveliness of your soul.

So weave into your life that which will bring about a pattern of great beauty, so that God's great tapestry will be enriched by the threads of your life.

THE BECKONING LIGHT

Beloved ones, allow me to guide you on to the path of divine inspiration where the light of God beckons you on. This path, where true knowledge transpires, can capture the mind of all who follow it. All along the way the soul will feel the need to reach out and cup the knowledge that is there for the taking, thus sharing that which God holds dear to His heart.

No soul need ever feel that life is without purpose, for the Great Spirit's creative plan shows that all His children have a part to play in the universal picture of life. God's plan for His kingdom is one that must be appreciated from a fine point of view, thus allowing us to understand the mechanism of His great mind. Then, and only then, shall we truly comprehend that which lies behind His dream for us all.

And so, beloved ones, on and on we must travel the road of divine purpose, knowing that all we learn is for the good of the soul, thus allowing us to grow and unfold in greater awareness.

Sadly, there are so many of God's children who are unaware of the truth that could set them free from the bonds of ignorance; thus their way of life is without the support of that which would uphold them when faced with the crises of life. There are those, too, who turn their mind away from the wisdom that comes to guide them whenever temptation holds sway. Alas, your world teems with souls who are lost in confusion, deluded by wrong beliefs. Therefore spiritual education must rank as the backbone, of society teaching mankind the elementary truths of life.

We, from the higher side of life, are only too well aware of the powerful influence material gain has over mankind, and therefore I say unto you, see the wisdom in seeking the treasure of the spirit, which can enrich and adorn the soul. You do well to remember, dear children of the Great Spirit, that material things fade away but the treasure of the spirit can be yours for ever.

I therefore beseech thee to ponder upon the words l have spoken, for l speak only in truth. My work for the Great Spirit is such that it allows me the privilege to teach mankind the basic facts of life and all they convey, thus allowing the soul of man to grow in wisdom and in strength.

Go forth then, beloved ones, and walk the path of the Master who brought his truths to bear upon you that man might gain insight into that which leads the way to the Father of all, Whose light beckons you on to reach the ultimate goal.

CLOSER TO GOD

Beloved ones, seek the light of Him who generates such power and who is the creative force of that which is good and beautiful; thus you shall feel the upliftment of your spirit as you draw closer to God. As you do so, so shall you touch the hearts of the paragons, the masters of the universe, who, through a long period of dedicated service, earn the right to serve God in a supreme way. These beings of integrity carry much wisdom, which gladly they impart to all who seek enlightenment; thus they reach out to guide you on to the path of unfoldment where the soul matures in spiritual beauty.

Much can be gained by seeking enlightenment from the learned ones, for they have experienced the height and depth of that which is bitter and sweet in life and therefore are only too well aware of the road one must travel to gain honour from God.

So, beloved ones, remember to be kind in thought and deed: as you sow, so shall you reap. Aim high when seeking enlightenment; thus you shall draw near to you Teachers of the Light, who will guide you forward, helping you to move closer to God.

THE LIGHT OF KNOWLEDGE

Cast your seeds of goodwill amongst those who suffer in ignorance, for they are the ones who need to be lifted up in the light of knowledge.

So many on your earth-plane are under developed souls who live a life of misconception; thus their aim in life is not of a spiritual kind and therefore is useless to the development of their being. These unawakened ones are empty vessels who need to be filled with inspiration, enabling them to rise above that which holds them in a state of materialism. We, who dwell on higher planes, pity those who are chained to the material things of life because we know they shall meet with a harsh awakening when the time of transition takes place.

To those of you who are enlightened and have gathered wisdom within your soul, I say to you, go forth and share that which you have gained with those who are deprived of such things, that they might appreciate the importance of that which lies on the other side of the coin of life.

Every child of God must learn at some time in their evolution that they are the weavers of their own destiny and therefore are responsible for the way it takes shape. But know this, dear children of the Great Spirit, not one of you needs to walk through life without direction, because Masters of the Universe await those who need assistance.

These paragons, who dwell near to the source of all life, seek to serve mankind in many ways. It is through their wisdom we can learn to climb the stairway of life to reach the planes of wonder and beauty.

Attunement with these beings can be achieved when the mind is in a meditative state, thus allowing the soul to transcend to a higher level of consciousness to link with the power of divine purpose. It is on this level the masters can communicate with those who reach out for enlightenment. Thus the soul is not left in any doubt when engulfed in the power these righteous ones bring, because it knows it has been lifted up into the light of Him Who rules the world.

But do remember this, beloved ones, no greater truth can one learn than that of knowing your thoughts, deeds and actions are recorded in the Hall of Reckoning and therefore will determine your next state of existence.

THE GEMS OF KNOWLEDGE

Seek you the power of the Great Spirit to help you fashion your life into one of perfection; thus the glory of His divine light will shine through your soul to touch those who are unawakened.

Many souls in your world are in a state of slumber, unaware of the purpose of their existence; how can they hope to achieve that which is so necessary to the soul growth?

We must endeavour to help them by stirring the mind into listening to the truth we bring; thus they will gain the enlightenment the soul needs to further its progress along the path of evolution.

Knowledge is one of the gems of spirituality. Its value is beyond comparison; it is the food that feeds-the mind, nourishing the growth of the soul. Without it man is starved of the vital ingredient of life, leaving him in a state of confusion.

And so, dear children of the Great Spirit, I say unto you, seek to learn all aspects of life; thus you will gain knowledge to help you understand the wisdom of the universe and the part you must play in it.

The awakening mind will feel the need to explore the depths of the soul, eradicating that which has caused it doubt; then and only then will it see the way to go, to learn the art of perfection.

THE TRUE WAY OF LIFE

If my words touch the hearts of only a few, then I shall be content in the knowledge that I have, perchance, opened the door of the mind, thus bringing about an awareness to help the soul see the true way of life, one that is rich in learning, giving insight into that which is relevant to soul growth.

So many of God's children are lost in a wilderness of doubt which can be so perplexing for them; thus it is my aim to lift these unfortunate ones from the perpetual dilemma they find themselves in and help them to progress in an enlightened way. I cannot over-emphasise the importance of soul development, which should be the prime concern of your daily life. Therefore I say to you, put into operation that which can strengthen the structure of your being to allow your soul to grow in a sturdy way. Be also mindful of the fact that by founding your growth on spiritual truths you shall not only enrich your life but will also free yourself from the bonds of ignorance.

But, sadly, it is true that so many in your world, and indeed in the lower regions of the spirit world, remain indifferent to the knowledge of eternal truths and therefore show no desire to follow the spiritual pathway. Content to reside in a state of illusion, they cannot see how fruitless this can be, and so progress for such as these can be long and laborious because they fail to see the light of reason.

But mentors such as I, who dwell on higher planes, wait patiently for these unwise ones to see the folly of their way and realise the quandary they are in, which is of their own making. It is then these souls are ready for direction, and thus it is with great joy we know the time has come to help these wanting ones forward to achieve that which their soul calls for.

Know this, beloved ones, not one of God's children need walk aimlessly through life. Knowledge awaits all who seek it and a sense of values can be gained by understanding the good principles of life. Blessed are they who walk in the light of truth, for they shall weave into their life the golden thread of spirituality, thus receiving honour from God.

THE STAIRWAY OF LIFE

Children of the Great Spirit, let not your hearts be troubled by the difficulties of life, for without doubt they come to test the spirit and therefore should be seen as valuable to you. Look upon the earth-plane as the schoolhouse of learning, where you are given opportunities to help you graduate to a higher level of consciousness. So do not shun that which may appear to be intolerable to you, for you could so easily reject vital lessons that need to be learnt.

Alas, it is true that many of God's children do not conceive the importance of soul development and therefore fail to progress in a satisfactory way. It cannot be over-stressed when I say attention should be paid to the spiritual welfare of your life, as neglect of this can only impoverish growth, thus preventing the spirit blooming in the fullness of time.

We, who come to aid you from the higher planes are only too well aware of the need for enlightenment in your world; thus we try to bring truths that will be helpful to you. Those who are wise shall listen and apply reason to the words that are given because our desire is to free you from false conceptions that would only mar your progress. To those of you who are ready to climb the stairway of life to gain insight into that which is relevant to your growth, we say to you, go forth, beloved ones, with the blessing of the Master. You can be sure his hand will guide you every step of the way.

GOD IS LOVE

Man, in the material state, cannot rightly conceive the true nature of God, for there is much to learn and understand about the Infinite One. Throughout the ages much has been based on theory when trying to analyse the working of this Great Mind, but none shall ever truly know the truth of Him until they reach the centre of divine power where all wisdom springs from.

It is there the true image of God shall emerge for perfected ones to see, but to reach this prime spirituality one must go through much purification, and this, beloved ones, could take a long, long time. But this need not be so if one learns to flow with the tide of life. Thus it is with insight you must see the benefit that can be gained by accepting with good grace that which comes to teach and test the spirit.

Time and time again you will find opportunities come your way to help your progress, and, remember, whatever task you may be asked to do, however small, try to accept it in the knowledge that you are being used by God to help Him in his work.

We know without a shadow of doubt that God is love. His love for us knows no bounds and flows through all He holds dear. Therefore, beloved ones, we must be careful not to suppress it by wrongful thought and feeling. He asks only of His children that they learn and understand the wisdom behind His creation and seek to find the part they must play in it.

Patiently, He waits for us to grow sound in mind, soul and spirit. We therefore must endeavour to be constant and true to Him Who gave us life that we might one day earn the right to dwell with Him in eternal bliss.

TREASURE OF THE SPIRIT

Beloved ones, be sure that your journey through life is secure by seeking enlightenment from the essential truths of life, which will stand you in good stead every step of the way.

It is strange but true that many travellers of the earth-plane form outlandish ideas on what life is about; thus they fail to progress in the right direction, which so often leads to loneliness and fear of the unknown.

We who serve God know from experience that sound guidance is vital to man's progress, therefore we offer words of wisdom to help mankind go forward in a constructive way. We cannot over-emphasise the importance of creating balance in your life to bring about unity between body and soul. Many of you neglect the spiritual aspect of your being and therefore find you are out of tune with the rhythm of your life, which creates disharmony and discontent.

Alas, many souls on the earth-plane prize highly wealth and fame, but these things will not grace the spirit. You need to put value on developing the good principles of life, to learn the true meaning of love, humanity, peace and goodwill. These are the gems of life and therefore are imperative to man's spiritual growth.

By all means enjoy the good things of life, but place them not above the treasure of the spirit. And forget not, beloved ones, that the gentle Father of mankind is ever present to guide you, if you would but ask the way. Never doubt the greatness of Him who holds you close to His heart. Remember, you are born of His spirit and therefore are a part of Him.

FOOD FOR THE SPIRIT

Capture within your soul the knowledge I bring to help you go forward with clear understanding of that which may have caused you doubt.

Ever in the midst of life is the Creator of all things, Who waits patiently for His children to grow in wisdom. He knows that each and every one of you needs time to learn the truth of life from the experiences you encounter along the way, and therefore makes allowances for mistakes made. But His children would do well to remember that God is not mocked. Those who take advantage of His generosity make a grave mistake and therefore will have to answer for the wrong they do.

But, happily, there are many of you who hunger for spiritual truths, but, alas, can be so often misguided by the ignorance of others, who can give false notions through lack of knowledge. Therefore I beseech thee to attune with the Masters of God"s kingdom in a meditative state of mind so that they might bring truth to bear on the golden plate of life for you to feed from. This God-given nourishment shall strengthen the fibres of your being, thus aiding your progress in a positive way.

Remember, beloved ones, the source of all life is ever watchful, moving in a calculating way, purposefully planning with precision the fulfilment of His dream. Therefore, we must respect this wondrous Spirit and appreciate that which He designs for us all.

How many of you look upon the experiences of life as stepping-stones to further your progress? Ye who are wise children of the Great Spirit know you are preparing for the great adventure ahead by gathering knowledge from the opportunities life offers you.

Therefore I say to those of you who lack understanding of spiritual truths and all they convey, delay not the search for the great literature of life which can broaden your way of thinking and which gives insight into that important region of your life that needs to be cultivated to stand you in good stead for the higher life to come.

Beloved ones, trust in the words I speak because my desire is to guide you, helping you to evolve to the glory of God.

THE GEMS OF SPIRITUALITY

Seek ye the gems of spirituality, for they will prove to be of great value. These treasures must be used with a clear understanding of their worth; they are God's gifts to us all to help us gain entrance to a fuller life, one that is endowed with much wisdom, thus enabling us to progress forward on to a higher plane of existence.

The light of the Divine One will shine forth upon all who seek to learn the truth of His creative plan, but, alas, time and time again, man is caught up in his own ignorance; blindly he walks through life, knowing not which path leads to God. Therefore he does not see the light ahead that is there to guide him forward to the door of enlightenment. And so I say unto you seek the pearl of wisdom, the gems of love, peace and harmony, for these are treasures that you need to help your soul growth.

We, from the higher side of life, bring you words of encouragement, for we know how difficult the path of life can be, but, dear children of the Great Spirit, you must try and cultivate the seeds of love, compassion, humanity and loving kindness within your soul; only then will you gain entrance to the door of divine wisdom, for there lies the answer to God's dream for us all.

VOYAGE OF DISCOVERY

Beloved ones, look upon the journey of life as a voyage of discovery where many truths are revealed along the way. Those who are wise shall heed the value of them, for they could be the lifeline of your progress. Remember, much awaits those strong in spirit who master the calling of the lower mind, which tempts its victims to turn away from that which could prove so fulfilling to them. Therefore, beloved ones, I say to you, have faith in the knowledge that, whatever difficulty confronts you, your strength of purpose can be the driving-force to steer you through that which could cause you defeat.

The Great Spirit giveth unto His children the means to accomplish that which they set out to do, but, alas, not all discover or use the treasure of the spirit which He provides for their need. Many travel foolishly along, seeking only that which gives material gain. But to those of you who are seekers of truth, I say to you, take unto yourself the gems of spirituality and cherish the meaning of them, because without this treasure you shall have nothing to grace your spirit.

Your journey can be one of great expectation of the good things that lie ahead, but if you fail to comply with the laws that govern the route you take, then, that which you find ahead will not hold joy for you. Therefore, dear children of the Great Spirit, I beseech you to see reason in that which I convey to you; thus you shall find the journey of life holds much promise.

So go forth, beloved ones, and hold the truth in your mind that I bring to help you reach the land of paradise, the summerland of spiritual beauty.

THE PATH OF RIGHTEOUSNESS

Beloved ones, be ever true to Him Who dwells in the light of eternal bliss, where the fountain of knowledge flows through the veins of the universe, inspiring those who are ready to accept the wisdom God offers His children to help them go forth on to the path of righteousness.

This path of true inspiration leads those who follow it to greater heights of manifestation, where the soul is refined by the nature of its quest to grow in spiritual beauty.

Life is a great disciplinarian, teaching us a mode of conduct that is relevant to the growth of the soul. Those who rebel against that which comes to aid their progress must be left to their own devices; thus they shall see how difficult life can be without the tools of wisdom.

No greater truth can man learn than that of knowing that he, and he alone, is responsible for his own soul development. Therefore he must learn to nurture it by good morality, knowing nothing can be gained by wilful neglect of that which is vital to the refinement of his being.

Capitalise on using the principles that offer scope to help you go forward in a positive way, thus gaining recognition in the eyes of God and in the eyes of your fellow-beings. By setting a good example you are showing others the way to the path of righteousness.

May the joy of knowing that you are the light behind another's step forward on to the road of discovery be your reward, thus filling you with a sense of satisfaction.

FATHER OF ALL

Hearken to the words I speak, for the message I bring shall fortify your esteem in Him who holds the world in His hands. This Master-mind, who planned with precise care the design of His kingdom, carries power beyond our comprehension. He is the mainstay of our existence and without Him we are nothing. No soul should ever underestimate His strength of purpose, for has not this wise and purposeful Spirit of Love fashioned a world to serve mankind in many ways?

Man has much to learn about this force that governs all life, this creative power Who has produced so much beauty. Behold it in the flowers, the trees, the sky and the sea, and in all creatures great and small. We must remember that God created them all, but, sadly, so many on the earth-plane abuse His work of art, thus tainting within themselves that which should be beautiful in His eyes, for the soul of man reflects the brightness and darkness of the mind.

But blessed are they who treat His work with reverence, because they shall touch the heart of the Father-God. Remember this, beloved ones, God is not mocked. Those who defy His laws or destroy that which He has created shall one day stand before Him in shame because they shall see themselves as they truly are.

So take heed, dear children of the Great Spirit, and allow wisdom to guide your thoughts and deeds; thus you will live in accordance with God's laws and life shall take on a new meaning.

So go forward with clear vision of that which I have brought to your mind. The way to God is just, and all who follow the path of righteousness shall truly be inspired by the light of reason.

Be faithful, be true, to the Maker of your being; thus you will walk in the radiance of His love.

POWER OF THE SPIRIT

Ye who have been moved by the power of the spirit, know how strong this can be, for it touches the core of the being and stirs within the mind the desire to find oneness with God.

Beloved ones, how joyous it is for one such as I who has travelled the road to fulfilment to see those of you who choose to embark on the path of unfoldment, where every step you take brings you nearer to God and merits you guides, whom He entrusts with his work, to help you move further into the light of that which is good and beautiful.

But we must look to those who have yet to experience the power that touches the heart-strings and brings to the fore the sweetness of the spirit, because many of God's children are void of expression and therefore fail to operate on that fine level of .consciousness so essential to the development of the higher self.

And so it is, with strength of purpose, that we who serve God bring power to bear upon these unenlightened ones by touching the heart and mind with words of truth to encourage greater awareness. But, alas, we know not all shall respond to the knowledge we impart; thus they stay in a state of ignorance.

Your world teems with souls who believe the earth life is the be-all and end-all of existence and therefore sadly neglect the spiritual aspect of their being, and it is with regret we must leave such as these to their own devices, trusting the time will come when the power of the spirit moves them to see how difficult life can be without the mainstay of that which is vital to the unfoldment of their being. It is then, and only then, that these ones begin to turn towards the light.

PEARLS OF WISDOM

Beloved ones, by the grace of God I come to enlighten your pathway. May the pearls of wisdom I bring beautify your soul growth, because it is God's desire that His children should derive benefit from the gems of the spirit.

Man, in the material state, often fails to appreciate the essential truths of life which are crucial to his development; thus the foundation of his growth may lack the stimulus needed to enliven the atoms of his being.

Through the ages man has created his own stumbling-blocks by failing to learn the wisdom of life; thus the path he travels may well prove an uphill climb. Therefore I say to you who are deficient in the knowledge of eternal truths, turn to Him Who holds the key to revelation that He might guide you to see the true facts of life.

God, in his wisdom, knows His children have much to learn from the great literature of life and therefore allows teachers of knowledge to descend to the earth-plane to help guide you in your quest for enlightenment. Much can be gained by listening to these learned ones, for they have experienced much from many lifetimes. Thus it is a great joy to one such as I, when invited to work with these beings of integrity, for I know l have then earned the right to do so.

And so I descend, with love in my heart, bringing you words of truth for you to learn from, and I therefore beseech you to value the pearls of wisdom that I convey to you because these are the gems which will shine from your soul.

BE STILL

Be still, beloved ones, and allow His peace to calm your spirit whenever the problems of life seem hard to bear. We from the higher side of life see so many of you lost in confusion through lack of understanding. You fret and fume, creating an air of uncertainty about you which disturbs your peace of mind. Therefore I say to you, seek the sanctuary of your inner being, where God awaits you. There you shall find sweet repose to soothe your troubled spirit.

The sanctuary of your inner being is the power-house of the soul, whence comes the strength to help you through the ordeals of life. This God-given power is the mainstay of your existence to aid you along the way. But, alas, so many of you are unaware of this force that generates such energy which upholds your flagging spirit, and so life for such as you can be an uphill climb. And so I say to you who are weary or on the brink of despair, turn your mind to Him who reigns supreme over all things, knowing all you endure is for the good of the soul.

Those who are strong will gain victory over that which comes to test the spirit; those who are wise will follow the light of reason. All must experience the height and depth of reality. Nothing is gained by turning away from the truth of life.

So go forward, dear children of the Great Spirit; let nothing daunt you, and may God's peace enfold you in the warmth of His love. Be still, beloved ones, and know that He is with you.

THE AWAKENING MIND

Be compassionate to those who have not yet reached the stage of awareness, for their life will be one of uncertainty. Those who are unenlightened cannot see the purpose of their existence thus they throw caution to the wind and behave in a most irresponsible way.

We from the higher side of life come to help such as these by trying to plant seeds of truth into their minds, but, sadly, we do not always achieve a rich harvest, for the minds of some are closed firmly against us and we must not force an entry.

We therefore must allow them time to reach that level of consciousness when the mind starts to waken from the sleep of ignorance to become receptive to the truth we bring.

Man's spiritual development rests entirely on his attitude of mind and the way in which he lives his life. All through the ages man has battled with his conscience. If he would only draw into the temple of his soul, he would be guided by the voice of truth that comes from the core of his being.

The inner voice of truth is the guiding light behind man's progress. Blessed are they who have learnt the way to God's heart, for they have shown perseverance.

And so, I say unto you, seek ye the door of your inner sanctuary, for there lies within a mine of information that will upsurge in the course of your attunement with the Great Spirit.

The enlightened soul knows no fear of what life might hold; he knows the hand of God will guide him through the lessons that he has come to learn.

And so, beloved ones, may the seeds of truth I bring grow in the mind of man, giving him insight into that which will help to strengthen and promote the growth of his soul.

WALK IN THE LIGHT

How blessed are they who walk in the light of God, for they have found the way to Him who is the power within all things.

The path that leads to the Giver of Life is one of much enlightenment, helping the soul to aspire to a greater level of consciousness; thus the soul will find in this state of awareness the desire to transcend further into the light, to gain wisdom from those higher beings who draw near to the throne of God.

These evolved souls have progressed through aeons of time, striving ever onwards to reach a state of eternal bliss. Words cannot describe the ecstasy of those who have experienced unity with the Infinite One.

The work of these great souls is to shed light and wisdom upon the universe, for they are the bearers of the Great Spirit's eternal truth that carries favour to all who seek to learn the art of perfection.

And so, beloved ones, I say unto you, open your minds to the knowledge that is there for the seeking. Open your eyes to the truth we bring; hearken to the voice of reason that comes to help you see things in true perspective. Thus you will gain advancement in your endeavour to reach the summit of spirituality.

And remember, too, dear children of the Great Spirit, the way to God's heart is in the learning to unfold the beauty within the soul, for there lies a pattern that is to be used to enrich the fabric of the universe.

SPIRITUAL ATTUNEMENT

Children of the Great Spirit, I say unto you, it is good to set aside some part of your day for attunement with the Great Spirit, the Creator of mankind and all living things, for all have a part in His divine plan.

We, by service and dedication, have been privileged to see but a glimpse of the tapestry of life; thus we learn there is a purpose in all His creation and we stand humble in His sight.

So I say unto you, do not be downcast when life seems full of woes, for from these trials and tribulations will come an awakening to help you understand the lessons you are here to learn. So go forward in courage, knowing you are guided by Him, Who is all-powerful and kind.

Christ came to teach mankind the principles of life, to guide him on to the right pathway, for all must learn and abide by the laws of life; no progress can be made without doing so. It is a great joy to us to see man seeking knowledge to enlighten his pathway, for those who seek will surely reap the reward to spiritual advancement.

The teachings of ancient wisdom will come to the fore in the New Age, bringing much enlightenment to mankind, enabling him to pick up the threads of life in a more determined way. The wise men of old did indeed leave a rich legacy, a treasure-trove of wisdom. From this knowledge will come a change of direction for mankind, leading to a more positive way of thinking.

And so, dear children of the Great Spirit, I leave you with these words of truth: it is well to remember your way of life is recorded on the higher side of life and therefore will determine your next state of existence.

My peace I leave with you.

THE DOOR OF REVELATION

May the words I convey sow seeds of understanding in your mind and may the love and peace I bring impart harmony to your soul, for, by the grace of God, I come to enlighten your pathway, by bringing truth and wisdom from the higher realms of light.

Beloved ones, I beseech you to see the beauty that lies within all creation, for the Divine Mind has fashioned a pattern that is truly one of great providence. God, in His infinite wisdom, knows His children must learn the truth of all He surveys so that they, too, can appreciate the value of His domain.

The working of this Intelligent Mind might be beyond our comprehension, but we do know His creation is one of splendour and all that He has created has a purpose and a role to play.

Throughout your life opportunities will come to help you to aspire to a greater level of consciousness; be ready to learn from life's experiences, for there lies the answer to your soul growth.

The door of revelation awaits those who seek to understand the way of life. Did not the master say, "Seek and ye shall find; knock and the door will be opened unto you"? It is through the door of wisdom that we meet the needs of the soul to help us progress further along the road of evolution.

And remember, dear children of the Great Spirit, to create harmony in the garden of your soul, for where there is peace the seeds of love will grow, bringing forth the
beauty that will enhance your spiritual growth, thus drawing you ever near to Him Who is the maker of your being.

THE LAMP OF TRUTH

Children of the Great Spirit, I beseech you to light the lamp of truth to help your fellow-beings find the path leading to God.

From the beginning of time mankind has questioned the purpose of his existence. Many have travelled a lonely road from lack of knowledge, thus knowing not where they are going.

Many wise souls from spirit have tried to break down the barrier of man's ignorance, but this is not an easy task when the door of the mind is closed against them and they must not intrude unless invited to do so. Thus man stays unreceptive to the truth they bring.

Opportunities to learn and achieve come to all, but many souls do not face the challenges set before them. They call defeat without attempting to try, and so progress for these souls shows little gain, but God is a loving Father and allows His children time to adjust, although this can take many lifetimes and much soul-searching.

God's dream involves all His children. Each one has a part to play in the universal plan. Into the fabric of His work of art are woven the patterns of each soul's progress; many will show great beauty, but, alas, some will be insignificant. The choice rests with us. God grants us free will, and so progress depends on our attitude of mind, the desire to learn and understand the wisdom of His plan.

And so I say to those of you who listen to the words of truth, go forward and fire the imagination of mankind with words of wisdom. All around you at this moment in time are signs of destruction. Your world is decaying before your eyes; the foundation of your life is being shattered by the ignorance of the unenlightened ones. The Great Master weeps for you all; He sees the mistakes of those responsible for the chaos that has come about. This bitterness and hatred must be destroyed to allow peace and friendship to grow between the nations of the world. Then, and only then, will you see a new dawning.

And so my peace I leave with you that it may take wing and fly into the heart of all mankind.

ONE STEP AT A TIME

Welcome, dear children of God.

I bring you words of encouragement to help you in your work and may the light of truth shine upon all that you do.

We see the light shining from your souls in the desire to serve the Great Spirit, but the path you have chosen will not be an easy one. At times your progress may feel slow but I say unto you, take one step at a time. The Masters in my world do not hurry; they have learnt from much experience to wait upon the word of the Lord to guide them. Let Him guide you too, and slowly but surely you will grow in wisdom, and knowledge will be yours to impart to others. Let not the harshness of the world deter your progress go forward in the knowledge that you hold the sword of justice.

Your guides, who have chosen to work with you, come in much esteem: they want you to trust their ability to guide you. They understand when you question their authenticity but I say unto to you, by their fruits you shall know them, for the knowledge they bring will be of value.

Abide, too, by the guidance of your earth teacher, for she has been privileged to help you and the experiences he has encountered will! stand you in good stead.

So, go forward in trust and soar to the height of your vocation.

THE WAY OF THE LORD

They who choose to walk the way of the Lord shall draw His light around them. His strength shall be their strength and His love and understanding in all that they undertake to do, because He knows only too well the discipline needed when one takes on service for God. To serve Him is a sacred thing and therefore should be treated with reverence.

Tasks for the Great Spirit may not be easy ones. One might need to battle against many conflicting conditions; thus only the strong survive and so it is with courage you must try to overcome that which could cause you defeat. If you are to wear the crown of glory for work well done, then that which comes to obstruct the good you try to do must be outwitted by a determined mind.

Beloved ones, because I have been privileged to bring my truths to bear upon you I should be failing in my duty ill did not caution you of the pitfalls of life that could so easily put you off course and thus hinder your progress. There are souls in your world who profess to be enlightened beings and, with honeyed tongue, preach the Word of God, but I say to you, always apply reason to that which is said and discard that which you do not feel is right. But you who are wise can do no better than to put your trust in the Lord, for the words He spoke were sincere and true.

Therefore never doubt His faithfulness to all who follow Him. He is a soul who has earned respect in every way and dwells on a plane far beyond imagination; thus you can put your faith in Him who can lead you to greater heights. So walk, then, beloved ones, the way of the Lord.

THE BOOK OF LIFE

As dawn follows night, so shall it be when man awakens from his sleep of ignorance to see the light of truth.

The Book of Life has many pages; each chapter shows the progress man has made from the beginning of time and, although much progress has been made, the laws of life have not been fully understood. The Great Spirit's laws must be respected and obeyed if the nations of the world are to come together in peace and harmony.

Through aeons of time man has gone against the principles of life; these treasures must not be lost, for their worth is of great value. One must seek always the eternal truth, for this alone will set you free from the bond of ignorance. Cast away seeds of doubt that come to destroy your beliefs, for if you believe in the words of the Lord, the Great Master of all time, you will not be misled.

He came to the earth-plane to teach man the fundamental truths of life. Believe in His wisdom. Did He not say, "Blessed are the peace makers, for they shall inherit the earth"? This is what your world seeks today, but, first, man must sort out the chaos that has caused so much turmoil; man needs the hand of friendship.

And so, dear children of the Great Spirit, let His hand guide you in all that you do. Live and work in love with a true understanding of another's needs; believe a new dawn will come to greet you, for the hand of time is indeed moving in that direction.

My peace I leave with you.

TURN TOWARD THE LIGHT

Go forth, ye children of the earth-plane, and allow the hand of God to guide you in your work.

The time draws near when you will put into practice that which you have been taught, and, by the grace of God, you will see the wisdom in the plan that comes about to your advantage, so turn toward the light, dear children of the Great Spirit, and you will feel the strength of His being.

Precious are they who follow the footsteps of the blessed Master, for they are indeed servants of God and therefore will be privileged to see the working of that great Mind.

And so I say unto you, rejoice in the knowledge that you have stepped further along the road than many, but remember to be compassionate toward those who have not yet been enlightened, for they are the ones who need your help. Many souls are on the first rung of the ladder: step by step we must help them to climb until they, too, reach a state of awareness.

Be ever aware of those who are seeking to learn the wisdom of the universe, for your mission is to guide and direct them. Many desire to follow the path that leads to God, but, alas, there are those who show indifference, so be brave in the face of opposition, for you will be opposed many times. But remember, beloved ones, your duty is to God and you must remain strong and steadfast in the work that you have chosen to undertake for Him Who is the power behind all things.

So go forth with courage, knowing your guides of great worth are there to help you. Trust in their knowledge, for they have walked farther along the road than you and therefore know how difficult the work for spirit can be, but we need your help. So many souls are waiting to learn the purpose of their existence, and so we must teach them all that we know, but they must be receptive to the knowledge we bring. Thus they will learn how valuable the lessons of life can be, for the light of truth must surely dawn at some time in their lives, giving them the encouragement to strive and unfold in spiritual beauty.

IN GOD'S SERVICE

Those of you who seek the light of God will be guided by wise souls who will help you find your true path in life.

How blessed are they who choose to serve the Great Spirit, and I say unto you, beloved ones, rejoice in the knowledge that you have reached a point in your life where you have become aware of the work that needs to be done for the Divine One.

We see the beauty that shines from those who are willing to serve; thus they will draw around themselves a band of souls who are like-minded, who therefore will guide and direct them in the work chosen for them to do.

The work of the spirit is never-ending, for your world is a tangled web of deceit. It cannot hope to function in a true and purposeful way until mankind seeks to learn the wisdom and truth behind God's Plan.

All around you are signs of destruction; man's foolishness will not bring him to the door of enlightenment, for he chooses to live in chaos.

And so, dear children of the Great Spirit, how joyous it is to see the light that emanates from those who awaken from their sleep of ignorance, for we know they will at last become aware and so will seek the knowledge that awaits them to help them go forward, and so like a flower that gently unfolds to blossom in beauty, they, too, will do likewise.

THE DOOR OF OPPORTUNITY

The door of opportunity is ever open to those who desire to follow the path that leads to God, for there lies the knowledge to help you see how wise and purposeful the Great Creator has been in the plan He created for mankind and all living things.

We who serve God have gained entrance to the door of divine wisdom, where plans of the universe are in great display; thus we learn the truth of His power and His love that is perfect in every way. And so I say unto you, seek the knowledge that will help you progress forward; by learning the way to spiritual progression you will know and understand how fruitful life can be.

But remember, beloved ones, the fruits of the spirit are not given freely: they must be earned by sheer determination and strength of character, thus giving you victory over that which can so easily sway the mind.

We ask you to bear with the problems that life can bring, for we know from experience that from the trials and tribulations comes an awakening to help you understand the needs of others, for all God's children go through times of mental anguish when the experiences of life are not understood, and so who better to reassure them than those who have undergone and gained knowledge of such things?

There are many enlightened souls in your world who have gained knowledge of true understanding, and so I say unto you, seek to learn from their wisdom, for they have much to give humanity and therefore will help you to advance in spiritual awareness.

Beloved ones, if you could only see the beauty of the crown that awaits those who are true servants of God and who have chosen to serve their fellow-beings, you would know how worthwhile service can be.

Blessed are they who bring joy where there is sadness, hope where there is despair, love where there is hatred, and peace where strife and discord prevail.

THE SCHOOL OF LIFE

Welcome, children of the Great Spirit. I bring you words of truth and inspiration, and may the path that you tread be one of enlightenment, leading you ever onwards in the knowledge that you will one day reach the door of divinity. The school of life can be a hard one but I say unto to you, value the lessons learnt, for they will stand you in good stead when the tests of life confront you.

Many opportunities will come your way to help you progress forward; accept them in the knowledge that they will bring you the experiences so necessary for your soul growth. God, in his infinite wisdom, knows His children must experience all aspects of life, thus enabling them to gain knowledge and strength of character.

We look upon your world of chaos and see so many souls locked in ignorance.The door of truth cannot open until they find the key of enlightenment, and so I say unto you spread seeds of wisdom that they might grow and multiply to feed the mind of man.

Reach for the light, dear children of the Great Spirit, for where there is light there can be no darkness.

Enter the door that holds knowledge of ancient wisdom. Your doubt and fear will dispel, for many truths will be revealed, and may your work for the Great Spirit be woven with threads of gold.

LIFE'S TREASURE-TROVE

Let the tempo of your life be one of tranquillity; thus you will find the peace you need to help you overcome the problems of life.

We see so many souls in your world lost in confusion; they fail to understand that living in a state of perplexity will not bring balm to the soul or create harmonious conditions for soul growth.

Throughout the ages man has created discord in his life. When will he ever learn to control that which comes to disturb the peace that is there to aid him?

Life offers many opportunities to help man learn and create conditions that will strengthen the foundation of his spiritual growth, but he must endeavour to overcome the errors of his own making; thus he will find the pattern of his life will take on a new meaning, enabling him to see the way in which he should go.

God bestows many gifts upon His children to use in accordance with His laws, therefore we must show gratitude by using them to perfect the beauty of the soul.

The purpose of life is to give you the opportunity to learn from the many experiences that life holds, enabling you to find your true self, but the soul must be tested time and time again until it reaches that state of awareness when it will understand the true reality of life.

Life is a treasure-trove of wisdom and enlightenment and God's children have the right to these gems of spirituality to help them evolve further along the road, to reach a higher level of consciousness.

And so, beloved ones, I say unto you, do not see your life as one to be endured: view it from the light of reason and a clearer vision will emerge, giving you insight into that which was thought to be meaningless.

THE LESSONS OF LIFE

Beloved ones, look upon the lessons of life as stepping-stones to help you forward on your path of evolution.

Many times in your life you will be challenged to endure certain lessons to test the soul''s capability. We ask you to accept them in the knowledge that not only will they enlighten your pathway but gain you insight into the reality of life.

Those who turn away in doubt cannot hope to gain a degree that will help them graduate to a higher level of consciousness. The school of life holds many opportunities for advancement, therefore I say to you pupils of the earth plane, use them to further your progress.

God grants all His children the key to the door of revelation but, sadly, so few seek that which lies within; thus they remain on a low level of consciousness, drifting through life in a most unsatisfactory way.

It is well to remember, dear children of the Great Spirit, that you alone are responsible for your soul growth, therefore it must be fed the food of knowledge.

Throughout the ages man's spiritual education has been ignored by many; thus they go blindly through life, not seeing how valuable this can be. Therefore, beloved ones, I beseech you to turn your mind to the truth I bring, knowing my words of wisdom will lead you on to a path of greater awareness, enabling you to walk with Him, the Great Teacher of all time.

BY THEIR TRUTH YE SHALL KNOW THEM

Let those who doubt the authenticity of guides be open to discussion.

We, who come from the higher planes of the spirit world, bring with us an aura of peace and power. We do not need to prove our identity: by our teachings thou shalt know us. We come to the earth-plane in true benevolence to teach that which we know will benefit mankind.

Your world has so many misguided souls who walk in grand illusion. They are not guided by teachers of high calibre: they allow those from the lower planes of spirit to influence their thinking and so mar their work for God. These souls, who come from the lower regions, do not have the experience from years of service, therefore are not spiritually advanced and will not impart wisdom so necessary to enlighten those who seek to learn spiritual truths.

And so I say to those of you who have mediumistic potential and are on the way to unfolding your gifts, test the guides by the knowledge they bring; by their fruits you shall know them and whether they are from God.

Do not allow yourself to be swayed by words of grandeur; they can come only to deceive. Your guides should be of gentle nature, forceful only from the power they bring. The words spoken should not be without element of truth; their duty is to guide you forward, helping you to unfold the gifts God has bestowed upon you.

Your earth teachers, too, have been privileged to guide you. Listen and absorb the knowledge conveyed to you; dedication and willingness to learn will bring forward guides of a high standard.

Do not try to hasten your development; it will only end in failure. Be patient; slowly but surely is the way to unfold, thus allowing your aspirations to come to fruition.

LOVE AND PEACE

Allow the pattern of your life to be one of beauty from learning and abiding by the laws of the Great Spirit.

I bring you words of truth and enlightenment to help you understand the way in which you should go to accomplish the needs of the soul.

Do not allow the unrest of the world to influence your way of thinking. Learn to compose your thoughts and you will find a greater understanding will emerge, giving you more insight into that which is needed to bring about a more congenial way of life.

Try to create harmonious conditions in your life by learning the real meaning of patience, tolerance and loving kindness; thus you will gain the support of those from the higher side of life, who will help you advance further along the path of enlightenment.

And remember, dear children of the Great Spirit, the precious gifts of life are those of love and peace and therefore must be cherished and used to help you unfold and perfect the beauty of the soul.

Love is the essence of life; it knows no boundary. Its ever-flowing power is ceaseless, enriching the life of those who embrace it.

Peace brings balm to the soul, healing that which causes pain; its soft caress brings serenity, helping the soul to overcome the harshness of life.

Peace is the outcome of spiritual unfoldment, thus helping the soul to transcend to a higher level of consciousness, to be closer with Him who is the Light of the world.

THE HAND THAT TURNS THE WHEEL OF LIFE

As the world awakens to the new dawn, clouds of darkness will drift away and man, in his new state of awareness, will seek the knowledge his soul cries for, but first he must clear the debris from his pathway, for the door of light will not open until he does so.

For too long man has had his way, destroying the Great Spirit's work of art, showing no remorse for the destruction of His work. We look upon your world and see such confusion, bitterness and hatred. This cannot go on: the wind of change must come to sweep away the chaos man has created.

As changes take place in man's way of thinking, true understanding will emerge between the nations of the world; enlightened souls will come forward with great knowledge. These chosen ones have learnt much from previous lifetimes; their knowledge and wisdom will benefit mankind in many ways.

The hand that turns the wheel of life will bring about a new dimension; young people will lean towards a more spiritual way of life, bringing contentment and a thirst for knowledge. Many will become the leaders of man and great spiritual teachers.

We see the advancing years bringing much enlightenment and man will move into a new way of life.

My peace I leave with you.

TEACHINGS FROM

MING FU

THE SEASONS OF THE SOUL

The unfoldment of the tiny being who enters the earth plane to begin the journey through life will be crucial to the character that will form under the guidance of the parents who have been chosen to help the soul on its rightful path.

As the infant grows and develops in the spring of life, impressions formed on the young mind will be of the utmost importance to the way its future life takes shape. Therefore, the teachings of good principles should be taught from an early age,when the mind is at its most impressionable, thus helping to stand the soul in good stead throughout life.

As the soul approaches the summer of life to stand on the threshold of discovery, the desire to seek and learn from the many experiences life holds will be eminent in the mind.

At this stage of life youth has a tendency to be assertive, thus feeling the need to challenge that which contradicts its way of thinking. But these tender years hold a wealth of learning, for the soul must find expression through experiences encountered.

The seeds of desire are strong in the time of summer growth and the physical life holds much attraction; thus the young souls can be easily swayed towards that which could be detrimental to the soul growth. These vulnerable and intricate years are not easy ones for the young soul as it struggles against contumacy; the need for independence and security must be understood by those who are responsible for the care of the growing mind. But, as youth approaches maturity and begins to take on the responsibility for its own way of life, progress made will depend on the way challenges of life are met and overcome.

The lessons of life are many but, alas, not; always understood, thus the seeds of knowledge will fall on stony ground, failing to enlighten the soul of that which it has come to learn.

As the soul mellows in the autumn of life, contemplation on past endeavours will no doubt take place, bringing an awareness of that which was not comprehensible in the time of summer growth. These mature years must not be wasted in wishful thinking or in past regret: progress awaits all who are willing to learn from the reality of life.

The trials and tribulations that come to test the soul's endurance should be accepted as educational and therefore need to be borne with courage and goodwill. Progress made in the autumn years will depend on attitude of mind and knowledge gained from past experiences.

Those who have sown seeds of generosity, tolerance, compassion and loving kindness will gain spiritual advancement. But those who sow seeds of indifference, selfishness and greed will not advance towards the glory of God; therefore the soul must learn to overcome that which dims the light within the being.

As the soul enters the winter of life to await the journey of great adventure, he who has been enlightened has gained knowledge of that which lies ahead; thus the time of transition will be one of joy.

Alas, the unenlightened one may find the winter years a time of wanting; failure to learn from the wisdom of life will not prepare the soul for that journey of greater awareness.

Much can be learnt and achieved through the seasons of life; therefore the soul must grasp that which comes to encourage the growth of the soul.

THE FOOD OF KNOWLEDGE

Look upon your journey through life as one of great value, for it will enable you to experience many aspects of life.

All God's children are given the opportunity to promote their soul growth, but if it is to grow in strength it must be fed the food of knowledge.

The Great Teacher who walked the earth plane so many years ago tried to feed knowledge into the mind of man, but so few valued his teachings.

Man's foolishness will not bring him the fruit of sweetness, neither will he gain from sowing seeds of indifference; the flowering of the soul comes from seeds of loving kindness, generosity, love and compassion.

The path of service awaits all those who desire to walk the way of the Lord, and we need so many willing souls to help us in our work. The light of truth must shine far and wide to help those who cannot see the path that leads to God. So allow the wisdom of the Lord to carry you forward, knowing that all you achieve in his name will be for the benefit of mankind.

Many souls need to return to the earth plane to accomplish that which they failed to achieve in a previous lifetime, and, although the school of life can be hard, the lessons learnt are of great value. Time and time again we must seek further knowledge, for there is so much to learn. On and on we must strive until we reach the door of perfection.

And so, my friend, see your journey through life as a great adventure from which much can be achieved. You can be sure that from the experiences you encounter will come enlightenment, thus helping you to gain a deeper insight and a greater respect for all things in life.

THE LIGHT OF TRUTH

Those of you who seek the light of truth will be guided by wise souls from the higher side of life who will lead you forward to the door of enlightenment. The path to God is one that brings many experiences, enabling you to learn the wisdom of life.

As you progress forward from knowledge gained, you will rise above the density of life to walk in light which will radiate forth to touch many unenlightened souls who seek knowledge to help them understand the purpose of their life on earth.

We must kindle the spark of light within their souls into a flame from words of wisdom, so that they, too, can enter the door of enlightenment. God gives all His children the ability to learn and unfold the powers of the spirit, but many fail to recognise this God-given gift and therefore do not see and appreciate the wisdom of His creation.

Those of you who do, create awareness that brings knowledge to help you understand the purpose of life and will enable you to attune with God and higher beings who will use you in service for the benefit of mankind, for many of you have potential. And so, my friends, let us try to help those in need; many are lonely, sick or sad, perhaps from the loss of a dear one, some are lost in the depths of despair from the trials and tribulations of life. They need the hand of friendship and a sense of direction.

We must try and assure them that from the dark clouds a silver lining will break through, bringing a new dawn to awaken hope and the desire to go forward in the light of truth.

WISDOM

The wise man listens to the voice of his inner spirit, for it is the guiding light that leads him forward into enlightenment.

But, to grow in wisdom, the soul needs to absorb knowledge from the many experiences of life. He does not argue with those who think they know best: he knows a still tongue makes a wise head, and so he goes quietly on his way, sowing seeds of truth for others to learn from. No obstacles will deter him; he knows the hand of God guides him.

The journey ahead holds no fear: he knows those who show courage, humanity and love will move forward in the light, thus promoting the soul growth.

Sadly, there are those who do not listen to the inner voice. They are impatient, rushing here and there like a whirlwind, disturbing the peace that is there to aid them. If they would calm their restless spirit, they would find wisdom comes from tranquillity.

So remember, my friend, it is a wise man who holds the key to the door of wisdom, for he has learnt secrets of the universe.

And so, in attunement with God, he walks the path of enlightenment, knowing the light of truth will guide and sustain him.

THE FRUITS OF YOUR LABOUR

Those of you who work tirelessly for God and spirit will indeed gather in a rich harvest, for by sowing seeds of goodness you will reap the reward to spiritual advancement.

The path of service is not an easy one, but by showing you are a worthy servant to God He will grant you the strength and stamina to go forward in your work.

Seek always the Divine Light; it will serve as a lantern to guide you, and even in the darkest parts of the earth plane you will be protected.

Many times in your life you will meet with troubled souls needing help and encouragement. Give them generously of your time, for some will need comfort from bereavement or sickness of the mind or body; others may need to unburden a troubled mind.

Pray that you might be used as a guiding light to heal and inspire them. You can be sure your guides and helpers from spirit will draw near to help and guide you.

The work of spirit is never-ending, and we need sincere, loving channels to promote our work.

So work on, dear friends. In the fullness of time you will rejoice when you see the fruits of your labour.

THE FLAME WITHIN

Bright shines the light from those who work in the name of God.

The path of service is one of dedication and servants of God must be steadfast in the work they endeavour to do. Wise are they who follow the path of enlightenment, for they shall unfold the beauty within their soul.

The passage of time brings many opportunities for advancement, therefore man must grasp that which comes to aid his progress. Time must not be wasted in wishful thinking. Life's journey can be a voyage of discovery, enabling the soul to learn that which will benefit his soul growth.

There are so many truths we wish to express to mankind to help him along the path of evolution, but we need channels who show stamina to manoeuvre our words of wisdom to those who need enlightenment. There are those, too, who need to be stirred by the teachings we bring; thus we must ignite and fan the flame within their soul to help them see the way to spiritual progression.

Golden opportunities await those who allow the joy of serving God to be eminent in their mind; thus they will aspire to a greater level of consciousness, to be met by those who work closely with God and the Master who tried to capture the imagination of man by his teachings of wisdom and integrity.

So go forward in courage and be true to Him Who is your guiding light. Have faith in your abilities; thus you will conquer that which you undertake to do.

Centre your mind on achieving the gifts of the spirit to help you in your work. Be enterprising and you will find your work will take on a greater level of attunement with those who direct you from the higher side of life.

And remember, my friends, bright shines the light from those who serve God.

THE FLOWERING OF THE SOUL

Soul growth likens to a flower, slowly unfolding from a tiny seed to blossom in beauty, but if the soul is to grow strong it must be nurtured from the principles of life and strengthened by many experiences. Wisdom will come from these fundamental truths to bring enlightenment.

The soul's progress depends on the strength of character; therefore tests of endurance need to be experienced, thus helping to correct imperfections.

All God's children are given the ability to reach perfection, but this can take many lifetimes, for one must learn the laws of life, but the laws are just and we reap only that which we sow.

The flowering of the soul comes from good seeds planted. By sowing seeds of loving kindness, thoughtfulness and generosity you will promote and enhance the beauty of the soul.

And remember, my friend, to tend your soul with care, for that which lies within is the power of your existence, the life force of all creation, and will guide you into the light.

CREATIVE AWARENESS

If one is to become spiritually aware, then thoughts created must be of good intention, thus helping to lay a firm foundation for the soul growth.

One needs to endure certain lessons in life for the soul to grow in strength. Wisdom will come from these experiences and will help you to understand the trials and tribulations in life.

Increase your awareness from meditation, and weave into the fabric of your life the beauty that you see around you.

Picture a garden that is dormant; imagine in your mind all that you desire to grow there. Be aware of the creation taking place from the tiny seeds you have sown and, as you see your plants grow and unfold in beauty, absorb into your very being the colour and joy they bring. Ponder upon the Devas, the tiny fairy spirits that tend the plants with loving care, for they, too, have a part in creation.

Above all, see God in all that you have created and be aware of His presence and the love and peace He brings, for is He not the Great Creator of all?

THE LIGHT WITHIN

All God's children have that spark of divine light within their soul, but if it is to radiate in beauty it must be fanned into a flame from lessons learnt.

Strive to overcome the obstacles that beset you, for one must rise above the dense things of life. Many times you will be tried and tested, but if you are steadfast and live by the teachings of Christ the light within will grow strong.

As you journey through life you will meet with many unenlightened souls, some living a life of selfishness and greed, some drifting into the mire. There are those, too, lost in despair, casting around themselves a cloud of darkness. We must pray for such as these, that they might see the error of their ways and the light of truth can penetrate the darkness, thus leading them forward on to the path of enlightenment.

And so, my friend, let wisdom be your guide; the truth sustain you. Keep the light within bright by service to God and your fellow beings, and the door of love ever open to sweeten your pathway. Remember, those who radiate light will never be touched by darkness.

JOURNEY OF THE SOUL

The soul enters the earth plane with vast knowledge stored in the subconscious mind from previous lifetimes. This knowledge will come forward in time of need, thus helping the soul to grow in strength.

The earth life is not an easy one, the lessons learnt can be hard, but it is by experiencing trials and tribulations, tragedy and sorrow, that we learn and understand the problems and sufferings of others, thus helping the soul to grow in wisdom.

At times you may feel tested beyond endurance, but God will never allow the burden to be too great for you to carry; He knows His children's capabilities and will provide the strength you need.

From the time you are responsible for your own words and actions you will reap only that which you sow. Good seeds planted will bring in a rich harvest.

If you desire to serve God and your fellow beings it must be done in love and true sincerity: false pretence is of no avail. Things that are done in service will show on the higher side of life, but that which is done for self will drop like the leaves from the trees.

Every chapter in your life will tell a story, from birth to the twilight years. As the soul journeys on, battling against the elements of life, it will need a firm foundation. Cultivate that of steadfastness, patience, tolerance, and feel compassion for those you meet on the way, for they, too, are doing likewise.

And remember, it is so necessary to teach the young ones in your care good principles. It will stand them in good stead throughout their life and help them to become worthy souls.

So journey on, my friend; seek always the truth and grow in wisdom from the lessons learnt. Knowledge is never wasted, for it is stored in the subconscious mind for future use, not only to help you but others too.

GIFTS OF THE SPIRIT

Those blessed with spiritual gifts should use them wisely. God bestows them for good intention; to abuse them for selfish reasons is wrong and therefore will not bring treasures from work that is tarnished.

The gift of healing is one of the highest forms of mediumship and can bring great joy from the knowledge that you are being used as a channel for the healing energies, to help those suffering in mind or body. Qualities needed for this work are those of generosity, sympathy, love and compassion, a truly precious gift to receive.

The gifts of mediumship are many; each one brings its own reward to those who use them for the given purpose.

Wise souls from spirit draw near to direct the instrument they have chosen to promote God's work. All they ask is that you provide a pure, clear channel for the work planned for you to do, and trust in their ability to guide you.

Those chosen to teach spiritual truths are indeed privileged, for the task they are given is to motivate the feelings and thoughts of souls who are ready to listen and learn. Even those who appear indifferent can be stirred and will ponder upon the words spoken at some time in their life. Words of wisdom are never wasted; they give much food for thought and lead many on the path to spiritual progression.

So many souls are lost in your world, searching for enlightenment, trying to find a faith on which to build their life. Some are tossed around in the storms of life; they need a sense of direction, a guiding light to show them the way.

And so, my friend, whatever form your mediumship takes, use it wisely, to the best of your ability, with love in your heart. Love is the key that opens many doors; it will radiate from your very being to touch those you meet on the path of life.

THE PATH OF SERVICE

Those who tread the path of service will grow in advancement; servants of God who choose you as their channel will come forward with knowledge to benefit mankind and will direct and guide you in the work chosen for you to do.

So go forward in faith; have the courage of your convictions that all will be well. The hand of God is in your work; He will not forsake you. If you find your work arduous at times, do not despair; the light of truth will beckon you on to fulfil the mission undertaken.

The need to awaken man's spiritual awareness is so necessary. The foundation of his progress depends on this, therefore knowledge brought forth must be enlightening and inspiring. Many await the light of truth to guide them; step by step we must lead them forward on to the path of progress.

The door is ever open to those who desire to learn the wisdom of God's enlightened ones. You will unveil secrets of the universe that will guide you in your work.

We know the path of service is not an easy one; it takes courage to pursue this chosen path, but if you persevere much joy awaits you. One day the blue bird of happiness will sing its sweetest song for you.

PERSONAL RESPONSIBILITY

All God's children are responsible for their soul growth.

The physical body is but the vehicle that we occupy for the journey in life; all that we learn is reflected on the counterpart.

We reap only what we sow but are responsible for our words and actions toward others.

Should another be unkind or indifferent toward you, send out a loving thought for them and pray that they will see the error of their way.

By showing love and care to others and sharing with those less fortunate than yourself you will set a good example for others to follow, thus creating the desire to learn the real meaning of personal responsibility.

SPIRITUAL PROGRESSION

Should one desire to follow this pathway, it must be understood that it is one of self-discipline; you will be tested and tried many times.

This must be so, if the soul is to grow the character needs to strengthen in the furnace of life's many experiences. There is no room for the petty things in life: one must cast out thoughts of envy, jealousy, selfishness and greed.

Virtues to cultivate are those of kindness, gentleness, honesty, patience and tolerance.

Above all, one needs to learn the real meaning of love. It is the essence of life in everything God created. To truly love is a noble thing.

And so, my friend, if you can stay the test of time you will be richly blessed. Should you falter on the pathway, think of the light ahead and you will be given the courage and strength to go forward.

A glorious future awaits those that reach the goal.